LOVE, CATS AND COWBOY HATS

First published in 2025 by OH
An Imprint of HEADLINE PUBLISHING GROUP LIMITED

1

Disclaimer:

Cataloguing in Publication Data is available from the British Library

ISBN 978-1-03542-585-3

Compiled and written by: Alison Maloney
Editorial: Saneaah Muhammad
Designed and typeset in Avenir by: Tony Seddon
Project manager: Russell Porter
Production: Rachel Burgess
Printed and bound in China

Headline's policy is to use papers that are natural,
renewable and recyclable products and made from wood
grown in well-managed forests and other controlled
sources. The logging and manufacturing processes are
expected to conform to the environmental regulations of
the country of origin.

HEADLINE PUBLISHING GROUP LIMITED
An Hachette UK Company
Carmelite House, 50 Victoria Embankment, London EC4Y 0DZ

The authorized representative in the EEA is Hachette Ireland, 8 Castlecourt Centre,
Dublin 15, D15 XTP3, Ireland (email: info@hbgi.ie)

www.headline.co.uk   www.hachette.co.uk

LOVE, CATS AND COWBOY HATS

THE LITTLE GUIDE TO
SWIFTIES

UNOFFICIAL AND UNAUTHORIZED

CONTENTS

Introduction

Taylor Swift isn't just a singer—she's a full-blown cultural phenomenon, and if you're holding this book, chances are that you are part of the magical world of Swift lovers! From her days strumming a guitar in cowboy boots to ruling the pop universe with *1989* and beyond, Taylor has spun lyrics into gold, and you've been there for every high note.

From her early country roots with albums like *Fearless* to her transition into pop superstardom, Taylor has consistently delivered music that resonates deeply with millions. Her ability to evolve, not only musically but also personally, has created a connection with fans that goes far beyond the songs themselves.

Her songs are the soundtrack to our lives—whether it's dancing around to *Shake It Off* or getting all up in our feels with *All Too Well*. Taylor's journey is our journey, full of heartbreak, self-discovery, and moments of pure empowerment. It's this realness that makes us feel like she's singing just for us, and it's why Taylor's tribe isn't just a group—it's a family.

Whether you've been belting out her tunes since *Tim McGraw* or you're newly enchanted by the *Folklore* vibes, this quirky little book is your backstage pass to all things Taylor. Packed with quotes that'll have you saying, "so true, bestie," fun facts that even the most die-hard fans might not know, and quizzes that will truly test your fearless spirit. Flip through these pages and relive epic Taylor moments, geek out over insider trivia, and find out if you're the ultimate fan.

So, grab your favourite pen (or glitter gel pens, let's be real), and let's see just how well you know the woman who turned heartbreak into art and made us all dance like nobody's watching. It's time to prove your status... *are you ready for it*?

Keeping It Real

We'll get right into it. By now you know that Taylor Alison Swift, born December 13th, 1989, is pop culture's queen. But did you know... Taylor has been staying true to herself since she was a little girl.

From the youngest artist to write a No. 1 song to the biggest pop star of the current age, what makes Taylor who she is today is the girl behind the music. The strength, substance, brains, and heart behind the chart-topping records is right here—ready and waiting to be heard.

"

All of my favourite people—people I really trust—none of them were cool in their younger years... It never mattered to me that people in school didn't think that country music was cool, and they made fun of me for it—though it did matter to me that I was not wearing the clothes that everybody was wearing at that moment. But at some point, I was just like, I like wearing sundresses and cowboy boots.

"

Taylor Swift
Vogue, January 16, 2012

"

No one gets through it unscathed. I think that's a hard thing for a lot of people to grasp. I know it was hard for me because I grew up thinking, 'If I'm nice and if I try to do the right thing, you know, maybe I can just, like ace this whole thing.' And it turns out I can't.

"

Taylor Swift
Rolling Stone, September 18, 2019

"

At the beginning of the year in seventh grade, we were all sleeping over at somebody's house, and they were talking about how they wanted to sneak over to this guy's house because he had beer. And I was just like, 'I want to call my mom! I want to call my mom!' My whole life I've never felt comfortable just being edgy like that.

"

Taylor Swift
The New Yorker, October 3, 2011

Taylor desperately wanted female friends at school but struggled. A painful memory is when she called some classmates to go to the shopping mall, only for each of them to make an excuse not to go. Eventually, she went with her mum and found those same "friends" there without her.

Now, Taylor has close friends in abundance, a "girl squad" that she cherishes, with celebrities like Selena Gomez, Gigi Hadid, Karlie Kloss, and others.

Literary references abound in Taylor's lyrics, from children's favourites to poems and classic novels—but not all of them are easy to spot...

Novel Inspirations
#1
"Wonderland"
1989 deluxe edition

Inspiration:
Alice's Adventures in Wonderland
by Lewis Carroll.

This book inspired lyrics about falling down a rabbit hole to find Wonderland, and meeting the Cheshire Cat.

Alongside singing and
songwriting, Taylor
is a talented painter.
Watercolours and
flowers are her favourite
medium and subject.

"

You are the longest and best relationship I have ever had!

"

Taylor Swift
To her fans at the 2013 Billboard Music Awards,
dailymail.co.uk, May 20, 2013

> Swift has created an unusually close connection with her fans by emphasizing that she's one of them and that they're all part of one big friend group.

washingtonpost.com, May 15, 2023

13

Taylor considers the number 13 her lucky number. She was born on December 13th, and she often includes the number in various ways, like writing it on her hand during performances in her early career or using it in her social media posts.

Fans write the number "13" on their hands during her concerts, to share the connection.

> **"**
>
> I was born on the 13th,
> I turned 13 on Friday the
> 13th, my first album went
> gold in 13 weeks.
>
> **"**

Taylor Swift
today.com, December 13, 2023

66

Fans are my favorite thing in the world. I've never been the type of artist who has that line drawn between their friends and their fans. The line's always been really blurred for me. I'll hang out with them after the show. I'll hang out with them before the show. If I see them in the mall, I'll stand there and talk to them for 10 minutes.

99

Taylor Swift
brainyquote.com

"SwiftTok"

The name given to the section of Swift-obsessed TikTok.

In this community, fans create Taylor Swift-related content, such as ranking her songs and reviewing her albums.

In 2018, Taylor Swift
bought a house
for a pregnant fan,
Stephanie, who became
unexpectedly homeless
after she was made to
leave her flat for health
and safety reasons.

Taylor told Stephanie: "I want you to be able to enjoy your little girl, not have to worry about all this stuff," to which Stephanie said, "That night she gave me her hand and lifted me off the ground."

The Independent, January 3, 2018

66

Country music teaches you to work. You hear stories about these artists who show up four hours late to a photo shoot. In Nashville that doesn't happen. In Nashville, if you go four hours late to a photo shoot, everyone leaves.

99

Taylor Swift
Esquire, July 7, 2023

66

I think the first thing you should know is that nobody in country music 'made it' the same way. It's all different. There's no blueprint for success, and sometimes you just have to work at it.

99

Taylor Swift
americansongwriter.com, December 15, 2022

66

I'm in the news every single day
for multiple different reasons
and it can feel, at times, if you let
your anxiety get the better of you,
like everybody's waiting for you
to really mess up.

99

Taylor Swift
bbc.co.uk, October 8, 2015

"

Every artist has their set of
priorities. Being looked at as
sexy? Not really on my radar.
But nice? I really hope that
is the impression.

"

Taylor Swift
The Guardian, August 23, 2014

Swiftmas

During the 2014 holiday season, Taylor sent surprise Christmas gifts to several fans, which was dubbed "Swiftmas" by the media.

She even hand-wrapped the gifts herself and delivered some in person.

Novel Inspirations
#2
"Love Story"
Fearless

Inspiration:
Romeo and Juliet
by William Shakespeare.

Taylor hones in on the love story
between the two main characters,
referring to herself as "Juliet" and the
love interest as "Romeo".

"

I try really hard not to take bad days out on other people. Because I will get asked for an autograph and a picture and there will be someone with their cell phone filming me in a restaurant. If I'm not in the mood for that, I just kind of stay in.

"

Taylor Swift
cosmopolitan.com, October 22, 2014

The friendship bracelets, traded by her fans at concerts, have become such a trend that even the British Royal Family are in on it.

Prince George wore one for the official photograph to mark his 11th birthday in July 2024 and his younger sister, Princess Charlotte, wore several friendship bracelets when she appeared with her mum at Wimbledon 2024.

Even King Charles and Queen Camilla have worn them!

"

I'm not naturally edgy, sexy, or cool.

"

Taylor Swift
cbsnews.com, October 29, 2014

In her New York apartment, Taylor has a Stevie Nicks Barbie doll that sits (still boxed!) in her kitchen. It was sent to her by the legendary Fleetwood Mac singer, Stevie Nicks, herself.

66

What I worry about is that I never want to end up kind of a self-centred, vain human being.

99

Taylor Swift
huffingtonpost.co.uk, August 14, 2014

Novel Inspirations
#3

"The Bolter"
The Tortured Poets Department

Inspiration:
The Pursuit of Love
by Nancy Mitford.

The narrator, Fanny, is nicknamed "The Bolter" for her tendency to abandon her family for her latest love.

Over 144,000 fans were so loud when Taylor performed for two nights at Lumen Field in Seattle on 22 and 23 July 2023 that it generated seismic activity equivalent to a 2.3 magnitude earthquake.

"

Unique and different
is the new generation of
beautiful... You dont have
to be like everybody
else. In fact I don't think
you should.

"

Taylor Swift

Taylor Swift Songbook (Guitar Recorded Versions),
Taylor Swift, March 2010

"

In fairy tales the bad guy is very easy to spot. The bad guy is always wearing a black cape so you always know who he is. Then you grow up and you realize that Prince Charming is not as easy to find as you thought. You realize the bad guy is not wearing a black cape and he's not easy to spot. He's really funny and he makes you laugh and he has perfect hair.

"

Taylor Swift
seventeen.com, February 14, 2015

66

At some point you grow
out of being attracted
to that flame that burns
you over and over and
over again.

99

Taylor Swift
USA Today, October 17, 2012

Novel Inspirations #4

"Lover"
Lover

Inspiration:
All's Well That Ends Well
by William Shakespeare.

Taylor makes a reference to the title of the play.

66

For me, when I picture the person that I want to end up with, I don't think about what their career is, or what they look like. I picture the feeling I get when I'm with them.

99

Taylor Swift
InStyle magazine, 2012

The Art
of the Craft

Behind Taylor Swift's chart-topping hits and mesmerizing performances lies a relentless commitment to her craft—her songwriting genius, musical versatility, and the intense training she endures to bring her tours to life.

From perfecting choreography to ensuring her vocals are flawless, Taylor's preparation for the stage is nothing short of extraordinary. It's no wonder that with such discipline, passion, and artistry, Taylor is not just a pop sensation, but a true musical icon.

66

I know the difference between making art and living your life like a reality star. Even if it's hard for other people to grasp, my definition is really clear.

99

Taylor Swift
goalcast.com, November 25, 2020

Youngest Grammy Award Winner

Taylor won her first Album of the Year Grammy for *Fearless* in 2010 when she was just 20 years old, making her the youngest artist at the time to ever receive the award.

"Easter Eggs" or hidden codes
left by Taylor in lyrics, videos, and album
notes are liberally sprinkled, and part of the
fun is working them out for yourself.

Easter Eggs #1

In the 2017 video for "Look What You Made
Me Do", a headstone in a graveyard scene
reads "Nils Sjöberg", the pseudonym Taylor
used as her song writing credit on Rihanna's
hit "This Is What You Came For".

"

I love to communicate
through Easter eggs.
I think the best messages
are cryptic ones.

"

Taylor Swift
ew.com, May 9, 2019

Novel Inspirations
#5
"So High School"
The Tortured Poets Department

Inspiration:
A Wrinkle in Time
by Madeleine L'Engle.

Taylor makes a reference to the young adult science-fantasy novel.

Taylor became a keen rugby fan after watching it with former boyfriend, actor Joe Alwyn, and his pals in a pub in London.

Easter Eggs #2

In the *folklore* lyric video, Taylor included imagery of a cardigan in a trunk, hinting at the release of merchandise inspired by the song "Cardigan" before it was officially announced.

At the prestigious Harvard University, there is a course on Taylor Swift in which her work is compared to that of the English poet William Wordsworth.

On the wall in her bathroom is a handwritten inspirational note that Paul McCartney wrote to her, taken from The Beatles 1968 song, "Blackbird", that says, "Take these broken wings and learn to fly."

Swift is known to show immense love to her fans.

In June 2010, she hosted a meet and great that was supposed to last 13 hours as a part of the CMA Festival in Nashville.

Almost 15 and a half hours later, Taylor was still interacting with fans!

Easter Eggs #3

In the music video of "Look What You Made Me Do", there is a scene where Taylor is sitting on a throne with the words "Et tu, Brute?" engraved on it. This is a reference to Julius Caesar and suggests betrayal by someone close to her.

Prince William and his children, George and Charlotte, enjoyed having a selfie taken by Taylor after watching her perform at Wembley Stadium.

Earlier, the future King was spotted "dad dancing", waving his arms to "Shake It Off"!

"

The scrutiny she gets, how much she has a magnifying glass on her, every single day, paparazzi outside her house, outside every restaurant she goes to, after every flight she gets off, and she's just living, enjoying life.

"

Travis Kelce
abcnews.go.com, 2023

"

There's a camera, like, a half-mile away, and you don't know where it is, and you have no idea when the camera is putting you in the broadcast, so I don't know if I'm being shown 17 times or once... I have no awareness of if I'm being shown too much and pissing off a few dads, Brads, and Chads.

"

Taylor Swift
katiecouric.com, December 6, 2023

66

Home is where the heart is, but
God, I love the English.

99

Taylor Swift
timeout.com, August 15, 2024

Kentish Delight in North London became one of the most famous kebab shops in the world after Taylor filmed scenes from 2017's "End Game" music video inside the takeaway venue.

She had been introduced to the shop by former boyfriend, Joe Alwyn.

ERAS
Tour Locations

USA

Mexico	Scotland
Argentina	England
Brazil	Wales
Japan	Ireland
Australia	Netherlands
Singapore	Switzerland
France	Italy
Sweden	Germany
Portugal	Poland
Spain	Canada

"

It's a goal
of mine to tour
the world.

"

Taylor Swift
bbc.co.uk, February 15, 2024

Taylor has kept personal diaries throughout her life, some of which she shared in the deluxe editions of her album *Lover*.

These entries provide fans with a glimpse into her thoughts and experiences during different stages of her life and career.

Taylor is a United States
history buff who enjoys
reading books about
the country's Founding
Fathers and the political
Kennedy family.

Novel Inspirations
#6

"The Outside"
Taylor Swift

"Illicit Affair"
Folklore

"Tis the Damn Season"
Evermore

Inspiration:

The Road Not Taken by Robert Frost.

In all these songs, Taylor references the road that is less travelled by.

66

I categorize certain songs of mine in the 'Quill' style if the words and phrasings are antiquated, if I was inspired to write it after reading Charlotte Brontë or after watching a movie where everyone is wearing poet shirts and corsets. If my lyrics sound like a letter written by Emily Dickinson's great-grandmother while sewing a lace curtain, that's me writing in the Quill genre.

99

Taylor Swift
lifestyleasia.com, December 27, 2023

Easter Eggs #4

In the music video of "We Are Never Ever Getting Back Together", the guy Taylor is breaking up with wears a scarf, and many fans believe this scarf is a recurring symbol from her relationship that is also referenced in "All Too Well".

Novel Inspirations
#7

"Cardigan"
Folklore

Inspiration:
Peter Pan
by J.M. Barrie.

Taylor makes a reference to the main
characters—Peter and Wendy.

Taylor's apartment in Nashville has a pond full of koi fish in the living room and a large 'birdcage' at the top of the spiral staircase, full of cushions, where she and others can sit and look out over the city.

The Swiftie Trail

Reading

Pennsylvania—Taylor's Hometown

Start your Swiftie trail where it all began: This small city and the nearby town of Wyomissing were Taylor's childhood homes, where her love of music first blossomed.

Drive through her hometown and visit the places that shaped her early years as she dreamed of becoming a country star.

Taylor loves movies and cinema, which is reflected in her music videos that often feature high-concept visuals and cinematic storytelling.

She directed her own music video for "The Man", and *All Too Well: The Short Film* won a VMA and was submitted for Oscar consideration in the short film category.

Eras Film

Following the commencement of
the Eras tour, Taylor released the
self-produced concert film, *Taylor Swift:
The Eras Tour*, on October 13, 2023.
Released in theaters worldwide, the film
contained footage recorded at the
Eras Los Angeles shows.

Rather than working with a major film
studio, Swift partnered directly with the
theatres to distribute and exhibit the film.

It became the highest-grossing concert
film of all time.

For the epic Eras tour shows, Taylor would rehearse the set list months before, while exercising on a treadmill.

She explained, "Fast for fast songs and a jog or a fast walk for slow songs."

Time magazine, December 6, 2023

66

I knew this tour was harder than anything I'd ever done before by a long shot. I finally, for the very first time, physically prepared correctly.

99

Taylor Swift
Time magazine, December 6, 2023

During the Eras tour, Taylor performed vigorously. She started performing three back-to-back shows per city—in Los Angeles, her final U.S. stop of 2023, she performed back-to-back shows twice in a row with only a day's break in between for a total of six shows in seven days.

In between tour legs, she would spend a day recovering, which she called a "dead day", to get ready for the next string of concerts.

"

I wanted to get it in my bones.
I wanted to be so over-rehearsed
that I could be silly with the fans,
and not lose my train of thought.
Learning choreography is not
my strong suit.

"

Taylor Swift
Time magazine, December 6, 2023

Easter Eggs #5

When Taylor stabs the cake in the "Blank Space" music video, it gushes with blood-red liquid, symbolizing her mocking the "crazy ex-girlfriend" persona that the media had created about her.

Novel Inspirations
#8

"This is Why We Can't Have Nice Things"
Reputation

Inspiration:
The Great Gatsby
by F. Scott Fitzgerald.

This songs makes a reference to feeling like Gatsby.

The Swiftie Trail

The Grammy Museum

Los Angeles, California

The Grammy Museum has hosted exhibits showcasing Taylor's career, with iconic outfits and memorabilia from her tours and eras.

Explore behind-the-scenes moments of her rise to pop superstardom and get an up-close look at some of her most iconic looks, like her *Fearless* and *1989* era dresses.

66

I think this tour has
really become my
entire life. It's taken
over everything.

99

Taylor Swift
eu.azcentral.com

The Eras tour is the first tour in history to generate more than $1 billion in revenue—the highest-grossing tour of all time.

"

They had to work really
hard to get the tickets.
I wanted to play a show
that was longer than they
ever thought it would be,
because that makes me feel
good leaving the stadium.

"

Taylor Swift
Time magazine, December 6, 2023

"

All I do when I'm not on stage is sit at home and try to think of clever acoustic song mashups and think about what you might want to hear. When I'm not on the stage, I'm dreaming about being back on the stage with you guys.

"

Taylor Swift
eu.azcentral.com

Easter Eggs #6

In the "Lover" music video, Taylor and her love interest live inside a house where each room is themed with the colour schemes of her past albums, referencing her journey through the different phases of her career.

The Swiftie Trail

The Kebab Shop

Hampstead, London, UK

A stop at Sunshine Kebabs in Hampstead, London, is a must. This is the very kebab shop mentioned in Taylor's song "London Boy" from *Lover*, where she sings about "walking Camden Market in the afternoon" and grabbing kebabs.

Visit this spot to relive her quintessential London experiences!

Novel Inspirations
#9

"Getaway Car"
Reputation

Inspiration:
A Tale of Two Cities
by Charles Dickens.

This song contains a play on words from
the famous opening line of the novel.

"

You've made plans so far in advance. You planned what you were going to wear. You memorized lyrics. You got yourselves here. You figured out parking. You figured out transportation, and I want to spend my hundredth show just thinking about that and living in this moment with you and being here with you.

"

Taylor Swift
eu.azcentral.com

66

[It] has definitely been
the most exhausting,
all-encompassing but most
joyful, most rewarding,
most wonderful thing that
has ever happened
in my life.

99

Taylor Swift
eu.azcentral.com

The Swiftie Trail

Bluebird Café

Nashville, Tennessee

It was in this café that a young Taylor was discovered, leading to her first record deal.

The intimate setting still holds live performances, and it's a must-visit for experiencing the place where Taylor's career truly took off.

> 66
>
> Nashville is my home,
> and the reason why I get
> to do what I love.
>
> 99

Taylor Swift
americansongwriter.com, December 15, 2022

Novel Inspirations
#10
"The Albatross"
The Tortured Poets Department:
The Anthology

Inspiration:
"The Rime of the Ancient Mariner"
by Samuel Taylor Coleridge.

In this poem, the albatross symbolizes
guilt or shame.

> Getting a great idea with song writing is a lot like love. You don't know why this one is different, but it is. You don't know why this one is better, but it is. It sticks in your head, and you can't stop thinking about it.

Taylor Swift
parade.com, April 25, 2024

The Swiftie Trail

Cornelia Street

New York City, New York

Featured in her song "Cornelia Street" from *Lover*, Taylor once lived in a townhouse on this charming street in the West Village.

The residence is now private, but fans can visit the area to walk down this picturesque lane and feel connected to the personal lyrics of one of her most beloved songs.

Novel Inspirations
#11
"The Best Day"
Fearless

Inspiration:
Snow White
by the Brothers Grimm.

Taylor refers to Snow White's house,
in line with her frequent references
to fairytales.

The Taylor Swift Effect

Taylor Swift's influence goes far beyond her chart-topping songs and sold-out stadiums. The Taylor Swift Effect is a cultural phenomenon that extends into fashion, social media trends, the music industry, and even politics.

Swift's impact is undeniable—she has a unique ability to turn personal experiences into universal stories, and with every album release or public appearance, she shapes conversations on a global scale.

The Taylor Swift Effect isn't just about fandom—it's about how one artist has the power to change the world, one song at a time.

"T.V."

This is shorthand for "Taylor's Version". If a song is mentioned as T.V., this means that Taylor owns the song herself.

At age 15, Taylor Swift signed with Big Machine Records: a deal that produced six albums and lasted thirteen years.

Although Swift owned the publishing rights to her music, the record label owned the masters (original recordings that were released to the public).

They refused to return them to Taylor unless she signed a new deal with them, which she refused to do.

Instead, Taylor decided to re-record the six albums (appropriately named "Taylor's Version"), along with "from the vault" songs that were never originally released.

So far, Swift has re-recorded four albums: *Fearless*, *Red*, *Speak Now*, and *1989*.

Only two more left to record!

Outfit Inspo #1

Taylor Swift
debut era

Taylor's first album was a country pop icon written during her freshman year of high school, back when she lived in Tennessee.

Think country chic with cowboy hats, sundresses, cowboy boots, and natural makeup.

66

I get so excited about
these things because
I love to dress up. But
I wear cowboy boots so
that when I walk down
the stairs I won't fall.

99

Taylor Swift
on the comfort of her cowboy boots,
Entertainment Weekly, July 25, 2007

"Taylurking"

This is a playful term coined by Taylor Swift fans to describe Taylor's habit of "lurking" on social media to see what her fans are up to. Taylor has been known to follow fan accounts, like and comment on their posts, and even send surprise gifts or messages to her fans, often after silently observing their online activities.

This interaction is known as "Taylurking", combining her name with "lurking," showing how closely she engages with her fanbase in a fun and personal way.

Rituals, Chants
and
Concert Traditions

Write the number "13" on your hands during concerts, to share the connection with Taylor.

You can add sparkly glitter to go the extra mile.

Outfit Inspo #2

Fearless
era

Taylor's second album was inspired by her teenage years, exploring love, heartbreak, fairytales, and magical lyrical imagery.

Embrace sparkly dresses, fun accessories, and playful, curly hairstyles.

> " I'd written so much tortured poetry in the past two years and wanted to share it all with you. And now the story isn't mine anymore... it's all yours. "

Taylor Swift
Vogue, April 22, 2024

"Swiftie Sleuthing"

The act of analyzing and investigating Taylor's songs, social media, and videos for hidden meanings and Easter eggs.

Rituals, Chants
and
Concert Traditions

When Taylor sings
"Bejewelled", shout: "Where
are you going Taylor?" just
before she sings
"I'm going out tonight."

THE TAYLOR SWIFT EFFECT

Outfit Inspo #3
Speak Now
era

Speak Now, Taylor's third studio album, is a true confession of emotions hidden away, now explored and brought to the surface as Taylor moved into her adult years, revealing parts of herself more personal than anything she'd shared before.

Stick to fairytale inspired styles, embracing the romance with flowy dresses and pastel colours.

66

It's pretty intense writing about my own life, my own struggles.

99

Taylor Swift
americansongwriter.com, December 15, 2022

The Swiftie Trail

High Line
New York City, New York

Taylor's song "Welcome to New York" celebrates her move to the city, and the High Line is a favorite spot of hers.

This elevated park running through Manhattan offers amazing views and a peaceful walk through the heart of New York, capturing the essence of her love for the city.

Rituals, Chants
and
Concert Traditions

Double clap during
the bridge part of
"You Belong With Me".

"Secret Sessions"

Special listening parties Taylor hosts for a select group of fans at her home or other private venues before releasing new music. Swifties who attend are called "Secret Sessioners."

"

Over 15 years later, Swift remains
at the forefront of delivering
fan-based experiences to cultivate an
ever-growing following. Whether it's
personal invites to the singer's house
for album listening parties, aka Secret
Sessions, or pre-show hangouts,
she continues to put her fans first.

"

independent.co.uk, November 17, 2021

Outfit Inspo #4

Red
era

Full of vivid imagery and expressive vocals, along with her well-loved humor and soft attention to the shades of love and loss, *Red* is an all-encompassing album of the very best of Taylor.

Pay attention to bold colours, edgy accessories, fedora hats, and red lipstick (of course!).

"

This process has been more
fulfilling and emotional than
I could've imagined and has made
me even more determined to
re-record all of my music. I hope
you'll like this first outing as much
as I liked traveling back in time
to recreate it.

"

Taylor Swift
on the process of re-creating her old music to reclaim
ownership, *Today*, August 10, 2023

Rituals, Chants
and
Concert Traditions

Turn on your flashlight
when Taylor sings
"Marjorie"—you'll see the
entire stadium light up!

Taylor Swift fans created a fundraiser for the victims of the Southport knife attack—they raised over £275,000 in just two days following an overwhelming show of generosity from the Swiftie community.

Outfit Inspo #5

1989
era

Moving further into her twenties, Taylor created *1989* as a multifaceted exploration of the complex joys and sorrows of life. Falling away from the heartbroken girl she once was, Taylor transforms through self-discovery, shaming the haters and allowing herself to be who she truly is.

Think 80s pop aesthetic with crop tops, sequin bomber jackets, high-waisted skirts, and different hues of blue.

66

No matter what happens
in life, be good to people.
Being good to people
is a wonderful legacy to
leave behind.

99

Taylor Swift
gofundme.com

The Swiftie Trail

Bowery Hotel

New York City, New York

This boutique hotel in Lower Manhattan is another fan-favorite location.

The Bowery Hotel was rumored to be a place Taylor stayed or spent time during her New York years. The chic, vintage vibe of the hotel has makes it a popular stop on the Swiftie trail, exploring more of her NYC hangouts.

"Rep Era"

Refers to the *Reputation* album and its dark, edgy aesthetic, which was a major departure from Taylor's previous albums.

Fans often discuss Taylor's different "eras" when referring to the vibes, looks, and themes of each album.

Rituals, Chants
and
Concert Traditions

As Taylor gets ready to sing "Style" at the concert, ask her "What time is it, Taylor?" She'll respond with, "Midnight!"

> **"**
>
> I'm just constantly in awe
> of our first responders,
> emergency workers and our
> healthcare professionals
> that are putting themselves
> in danger every single day.
>
> **"**

Taylor Swift
nme.com, April 5, 2020

THE TAYLOR SWIFT EFFECT

Outfit Inspo #6

Reputation
era

Moving away from the constant optimism and innocence of previous albums, Swift breaks away from the usual reputation into a bolder, fiercer version of herself in *Reputation*.

Embrace dark and dramatic outfits, with black and metallic tones, and statement accessories.

GoFundMe had to raise its donation limit after Taylor Swift generously pledged $50,000 to support an 11-year-old fan battling leukemia.

Swift, known for her heartfelt gestures toward fans, wanted to help cover the young girl's medical expenses.

The Swiftie Spirit

Here are some of the unique traits that make up the heart and soul of a Swiftie.

1. Passionate Devotion

Swifties are fiercely loyal to Taylor and her music.

2. Detail-Oriented

Swifties are known for their ability to spot even the smallest Easter eggs, hidden meanings, and references in Taylor's music.

3. Creative and Expressive

Swifties channel their creativity in ways that celebrate their love for Taylor's music.

4. Empathetic and Supportive

Swifties are deeply empathetic and support each other, creating a positive and inclusive space for fans.

5. Inclusive and Diverse

The Swiftie community is broad and diverse, with people from all over the world and from different walks of life.

6. Resilient and Protective

Swifties have seen Taylor go through public ups and downs, and they remain steadfast in their support.

7. Engaged and Interactive

Swifties attend concerts, join online fan clubs, and even engage in trending conversations about Taylor.

8. Emotional Connection

Swifties feel a deep emotional connection to Taylor's music, with songs that speak to their personal experiences, from heartbreak to joy.

9. Adaptable and Growth-Oriented

Swifties embrace Taylor's evolution as an artist and appreciate her versatility and growth, and grow along with her.

10. Community-Building Spirit

Swifties take pride in the positive and welcoming nature of their community, creating lasting friendships through their shared love for Taylor Swift.

"Sad Girl Autumn"

A phrase associated with the melancholy tone of Taylor's *Folklore* and *Evermore* albums, which contain more introspective, sad, and autumnal songs.

Rituals, Chants
and
Concert Traditions

At the start of "Delicate",
right after Taylor sings
"But you can make me a drink",
yell "One, two, three, let's go!"

Outfit Inspo #7

Lover
era

A beautiful, all-encompassing album of all things love: the good and the bad. *Lover* is a bright, fun, and whimsical love letter to the feeling that surrounds us all.

Outfits should be dreamy, soft, and playful, with floral patterns and pastel colours.

The Swiftie Trail

The Feathers Pub

Camden, London, UK

In "London Boy", Taylor mentions sipping tea at a pub in Camden. Though it may not be the exact pub, fans have narrowed it down to The Feathers Pub in Camden as a possible spot.

While in Camden, explore the vibrant market district that Taylor sings about.

Taylor Swift wrote and released the song "Ronan" in honor of a young boy named Ronan, whose fight against neuroblastoma was chronicled by his mother, Maya, in a blog.

In September 2012, Taylor—then primarily a country artist—performed the song during the Stand Up to Cancer event and pledged all proceeds from the track to cancer-related charities.

"

In my opinion, one of the bravest things that a human being could ever do is to go through something absolutely unbearable and then share their experience with the world. There's a woman here tonight named Maya Thompson and I wouldn't know half as much as I know about childhood cancer and childhood cancer research if she hadn't shared her story about her son Ronan.

"

Taylor Swift
usmagazine.com, August 18, 2015

Outfit Inspo #8

Folklore and *Evermore* eras

Two albums intertwined with overarching storylines, *Folklore* and *Evermore* are twins to each other, exploring themes of hurt and healing.

Embrace fairytale-core with earthy tones, vintage dresses, and cosy, warm knitwear.

Rituals, Chants
and
Concert Traditions

When Taylor sings "I Can
Do It With A Broken Heart", she'll
say the line "As the crowd was
chanting more." When she says
this, shout "more!"

> **"**
>
> I have cats. I'm obsessed with them… They're very dignified. They're independent. They're very capable of dealing with their own life.
>
> **"**

Taylor Swift
Time magazine, April 24, 2019

"Kitty Committee"

Refers to Taylor's beloved cats—Meredith, Olivia, and Benjamin.

Swifties love discussing them and any references Taylor makes to her cats in social media or interviews.

Rituals, Chants
and
Concert Traditions

Before Taylor sings "Lord, save me, my drug is my baby" during the song "Don't Blame Me', shout "Take us to church!"

The Swiftie Trail

The 13 Wall

Nashville, Tennessee

Back in Nashville, the 13 Wall in The Gulch neighborhood is a vibrant, fan-created mural that celebrates Taylor's favorite number, 13.

Take a photo in front of this iconic spot and leave your mark on the Nashville scene!

Outfit Inspo #9

Midnights
era

Her 10th album to date, *Midnights*, returns to the pop that Taylor is so well-known for.

Embracing contrasts, in life and within herself, this album is a reflection on the good and dark moments that we all experience.

Think all things glamorous and mysterious, with gold accessories and elegant dresses in moody colours.

Rituals, Chants
and
Concert Traditions

During "Blank Space",
as Taylor sings "And I'll write
your name", get ready to
chant the name of your city.

"Scarf Gate"

A term used for the ongoing fan fascination with the scarf referenced in "All Too Well".

It has taken on a life of its own, representing emotional baggage from past relationships.

"

The scarf is a metaphor... We turned it red because red is a very important colour in this album, which is called *Red*.

"

Taylor Swift
on the significance of the scarf, buzzfeednews.com,
September 12, 2022

Taylor Trivia

Think you know everything about Taylor Swift? From her earliest country hits to her latest chart-toppers, Taylor's career is filled with unforgettable moments, iconic lyrics, and standout performances.

But beyond the fame, there's the real Taylor—cat lover, baking enthusiast, and avid reader—who lives a life full of simple joys and personal passions.

It's time to prove how well you know the woman behind the spotlight!

In which 2014 sci-fi movie did Taylor have a supporting role?

Answer: The Giver

What was the name of
the record label
she signed with at the
age of 15?

Answer: Big Machine Records

Taylor is the first women to appear twice on a prestigious *Time* magazine "Person of the Year" cover during which two years?

Answer: 2017 and 2023

When she was 14, Taylor wrote a novel about a mother who wants a son but instead has a girl. What was it called?

Which country and western star once said: "Taylor Swift is the greatest thing that's ever happened to country music"?

Answer: Dolly Parton

What is Taylor's lucky number and why?

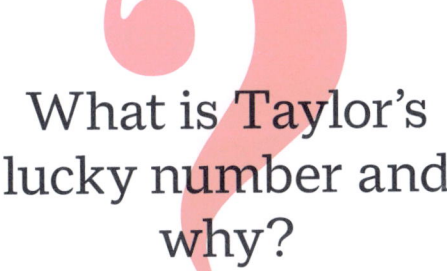

When asked what superpower she would like to have, what did Taylor choose?

Answer: Healing people

What nickname does
Taylor's brother Austin
use to call her?

While she was still at school, Taylor bought a car with the money she had earned from song writing—a silver Lexus SC430. Why did she choose this model?

Answer: It was the same car that Regina George drove in the film Mean Girls

What is the first song
that Taylor learnt to play
on the guitar?

Answer: "Kiss Me" by Sixpence None the Richer

What did Taylor say
was her spirit animal
and why?

Answer: Dolphins, because they are social animals

Who did Taylor write the song "The Best Day" about?

TAYLOR TRIVIA

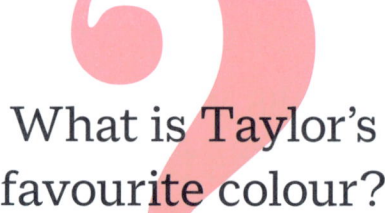

What is Taylor's favourite colour?

Answer: Purple

158

At age 15, Taylor took a picture of a Hollywood actress wearing a pink dress to several clothes stores in the hope that they had something similar. Which actress was it?

What was the name of
the first perfume that
Taylor released?

In the title track of the album *The Tortured Poets Department*, Taylor references which famous Welsh poet from the past?

At her beach home in Rhode Island, Taylor said there was a seagull that liked to cool off in her pool. What did she name it?

Answer: George Washington

Which book did Taylor enjoy reading so much that she finished reading it in two days?

Taylor's parents have videos of her on the beach going up to different people and singing them songs from which Disney musical?

Taylor has a great collection of coffee mugs at home. Which animal is printed on these mugs?

Taylor modelled for which fashion house's "Rising Stars" campaign in 2003?

What is Taylor's favourite gemstone?

Star-Studded Praise

Taylor Swift has not only captured the hearts of millions of fans around the world, but she's also earned the admiration and respect of her peers.

From fellow musicians to actors and industry legends, Taylor's talent, work ethic, and influence have made a lasting impact on everyone she's crossed paths with.

Dive into the words of celebrities who have praised Taylor's songwriting genius, her fearless authenticity, and her kindness behind the scenes.

66

Taylor is a very talented girl
and she's productive and keeps
coming up with great concepts
and songs, and she's huge.
She knows music, and she knows
how to write. She's like that
generation's Beatles.

99

Billy Joel
New York Post, December 30, 2021

> 66
>
> She's super talented...
> a tremendous writer.
>
> 99

Bruce Springsteen
MetalCastle, November 2, 2022

"

She's really talented and beautiful.

"

Diana Ross
Glamour, November 19, 2017

❝

I love Taylor Swift.
I think she's adorable.
Her music makes me so
happy. She's very level-
headed. She's a very, very
smart girl. Very wise.

❞

Britney Spears
Billboard, August 18, 2015

66

Taylor Swift is going to
be here for as long as
she chooses to be. She's
growing as a person. She's
growing as an artist.

99

Jon Bon Jovi
Rolling Stone, October 2, 2010

66

I think she moves economies. She changes the way the world works, and that's amazing.

99

Michael J. Fox
NME, April 17, 2024

"

She's so lovely. She's so sweet. Everything that comes across in her music is warm. Her personality, her charm. She's just an angel. I just really like her a lot.

"

Zac Efron
OK! magazine, March 5, 2012

> **"**
> I think Taylor's one of
> the greatest songwriters
> of our generation.
> And she's fun, as well.
> **"**

Adele
Billboard, October 26, 2022

"

I've been a Taylor Swift fan for as long as I can remember. But it wasn't until I met and got to know her that I understood how wonderful a person she truly is... Taylor makes the job of creating music for millions of people look easy. It all comes from her—her belief in magic and love, and her ability to be as honest and raw as possible... It's so rare and so special.

"

Shawn Mendes
Time magazine, April 29, 2019

I love Taylor Swift.

Ringo Starr
Far Out magazine, March 23, 2022

"

Taylor is a sweetheart. Very,
very sweet, very, very genuine,
extremely generous, picks up the
phone every time I call her.
My mom doesn't even always
pick up the phone!

"

Kesha
Glamour, October 4, 2017

"

Over the years I have known some great songwriters, and I have also known great singers and performers. It's rare to see all those talents in one person—Taylor Swift. Her lyrics resonate across all generations, her songs touch everyone and her impact around the world is extraordinary.

"

Carole King
Rolling Stone, October 30, 2021

> 66
>
> Taylor has such an amazing stage presence, and she really connects with her fans.
>
> 99

Mick Jagger

66

She writes some damn
catchy pop songs. I can't
get them out of my head.

99

Madonna
Us Weekly, February 9, 2015

"

In my mind, she's a role model.

"

Rihanna
NME, September 17, 2015

"

She's one of the people who is really supporting women in the entertainment business. It's really inspiring to see that, and I think that it's kind of what we want to share with our generation.

"

Gigi Hadid
The Talko, September 11, 2015

66

She's really funny.
She's got a very British
sense of humour. We love
doing scenes from
The Office.

99

Ellie Goulding
Evening Standard, October 30, 2015

66

She's magnificent.

99

Henry Cavill
E! News, March 28, 2024

66

She's really kind of just normal and sweet.

99

Channing Tatum
People magazine, August 17, 2024

66

No matter what people are
saying, everything that
I've ever seen her tackle,
she's done with grace.

99

Sabrina Carpenter
Marie Claire, August 24, 2024

66

I'm a Swiftie, too.

99

Jennifer Lopez
Daily Mail, December 13, 2023

66

I absolutely adore her.

99

Kate Hudson
People magazine, June 12, 2024

66

She is just one of those rare timeless artists who gets it right every time. She's an absolute powerhouse.

99

RAYE
Us Weekly, June 7, 2024